# THE BIOLOGICAL BASIS OF RELIGION AND GENIUS

*GOPI KRISHNA*

An Appeal to World Leaders,
Scientists and Scholars

# THE BIOLOGICAL BASIS OF RELIGION AND GENIUS

by Gopi Krishna

NC PRESS, INC., NEW YORK

Published by NC Press, Inc. New York, New York for Kundalini Research
Foundation, 440 East 62nd Street, New York, New York 10021 and the
Research Institute for Kundalini, Srinagar, Kashmir, India.

*"If any man will do His will, he shall know of the doctrine . . . and ye shall know the truth, and the truth shall make you free."*

St. John, Chaps. 7 and 8

# Contents

# PREFACE

ON THE BASIS OF MY OWN EXPERIENCE, extending to more than thirty years, I have come to the conclusion that mankind is slowly evolving towards a sublime state of consciousness of which fleeting glimpses have been afforded to us by all great seers and mystics of the past and present.

There is no doubt that some of the leading intellectuals of this era accept the existence of an evolutionary impulse in the race, but the ultimate goal and the modus operandi of the impulse—according to them—are still shrouded in mystery.

The purport of this work—which is only an introduction to the work that is to follow—is that there is a specific psychosomatic power center in man, and that it is by the action of this center that human evolution has proceeded so far. This Divine organ is naturally active in born sages, mystics, prophets and all men of genius and can be roused to activity with appropriate methods in those already advanced on the path of evolution.

This power center, known in India by the name of Kundalini, has been used for the attainment of higher consciousness from times immemorial. In fact, there is every reason to believe that the extraordinary exuberance of religious genius in India in the Vedic Age—which was never surpassed in any subsequent epoch—was due to an intimate knowledge of this mighty mechanism, coupled with a social order more in harmony with evolutionary laws.

The existence of the power center and methods to rouse it were known in almost all ancient cultures of Asia, Europe, America and even in Africa. I believe that a voluntary arousal of Kundalini, under satisfactory conditions and observed by competent investigators, can furnish *unquestionable proof* of the existence of this center in the body and its capacity to bestow psychic gifts, genius and cosmic consciousness.

The experiments, when proved empirically, would effect a radical change in some current concepts about life and narrow the gulf existing between religion and science. It would also draw the attention of scholars towards the spiritual laws of evolution of which they have no knowledge at present.

In this brief summary the consequences of a collective breach of these laws are outlined. There is nothing haphazard and arbitrary in the universe, and there are as effective and as inviolable laws in the spiritual realm as there are in the physical world. The present explosive situation in the world is due to a serious violation of these laws.

At the present stage of evolution, the leading intellects of the earth—with proper efforts done in suitable environments—can in a fair percentage of cases succeed in arousing Kundalini and by this agency win access to a higher realm of consciousness. The supersensory plane of knowledge will be a necessary endowment of the luminaries who will guide the race in the foreseeable future.

It was the possession of this supersensory channel of cognition that gave to all great seers and prophets such deep knowledge of human nature and such farsightedness. The knowledge of the evolutionary laws and the goal of human progress bring to the fore-front the need for mental hygiene as essential as the hygiene of the body. With the necessary precautions taken, it will be possible in the time to come, I believe, to control and eliminate war, just as mankind has already learned to control scourges such as cholera, plague and smallpox.

Gopi Krishna
Srinagar, Kashmir—February, 1971

# I.

# THE SHORT FALL
# OF RELIGION

THE PHENOMENON OF RELIGION IS A MYSTERY which so far has
baffled all attempts for a solution. There can be no denying the
fact that from prehistoric times, as far back as modern investigators have been able to trace, man has always been in possession
of a religion of some sort. Excavations of fossils of even the earlier
Stone Age reveal ceremonial burials, thus furnishing evidence
for the fact that, even in the primitive state of culture, belief in
survival and the nature of the soul as an entity, separate and distinct from the body, was prevalent in various forms among the
savage populations of the earth. From the study of primitive religions and cults, made by scholars, it is obvious beyond doubt that

1

the savage faiths were more or less a bundle of superstition, myth, and ritual which not infrequently assumed horrible and fantastic form. Human sacrifice, sexual orgies, and dreadful forms of self-torture were not infrequently the common features of the methods of worship of these prehistoric creeds.

In less developed nations and even in some advanced societies we still come across surviving remnants of these hideous practices of the past. Until very recent times voluntary castration was prevalent among some categories of priests, and fearful instances of human sacrifice come every now and then to the notice of the shocked public of some countries. Among the isolated savage populations of Africa and Australia, the odious practices and rituals of primitive cults persist to this day. Not infrequently, revolting accounts of these quaint and repellent religious practices appear in well-known journals and newspapers of the world.

It is possible that the reader might be expecting something about the holy and the sublime, and my introduction of the subject by allusion to the hideous practices of the past might appear to some of them as ill-timed and irrelevant to the subject in hand. About this I beg to say that it is precisely because we have failed to study religion as a whole, from the earliest vestiges of it to the present lofty ideals of the prophets and the sages, not only in the case of one but all the religions of the earth taken as one composite whole, that we have so far not been able to discover the mighty law of nature underlying all the infinitely varied manifestations of religion and the religious impulse from prehistoric times to the present day. This law is as operative now, when the world is sharply divided between those who believe in the existence of God and those who do not, as it was when religion occu-

2

pied a position of supremacy in many parts of the world, and even kings had to bow to the dictates of the Church.

I may be pardoned if I request the reader to put one simple question to himself, and that question is why do we believe at all in the existence of an Omniscient and Omnipotent Divine Power that has brought this world and ourselves into existence, when we can find no evidence, perceptible to the senses, to prove conclusively that such a Power exists at all? And why do we strive for perfection and a better order of things when, from a study of the past and our own experience of the present, we are irresistibly drawn to the conclusion that from the earliest epochs not only the earth but even the seas have been a battleground for a ruthless struggle for existence in which neither God nor any supernatural agency ever intervened to grant victory or even protection to the believers against those who did not believe in God or a higher order of existence? The question I pose is as old as humanity itself, and to this day no satisfactorily convincing answer has been given by any authority on religion or by an illumined sage, ancient or modern. Had this question been effectively answered at any time in the long history of mankind, the division between believers and nonbelievers or between the devout and the skeptics would have ceased to exist there and then; nor would religion have lost her ascendancy or suffered such reverses and upheavals as it has in this enlightened age.

It is now too late in the day to ascribe all religious phenomena and the existence of the religious impulse in man to the Will of God as the preachers of religion often attempt to do. It is also too late in the day to say that man is religious because God, who is pure spirit, is filled with desire that he should worship

Him and seek Him amid all the temptations of the flesh, in order to attain perennial peace and happiness in the Hereafter. The battle for salvation, which almost all religions of mankind impose on their followers, demands that the seeker must renounce the pleasures of earth to gain those of Heaven after death. But what the blessings of Heaven are and what exactly the state of man would be after his departure to the other world are enigmas that no one to this day has satisfactorily solved.

Even among orthodox believers of the various religions there is no concord as to what form the surviving soul would take after death to gain the promised reward for his heroic battle on earth against temptations to win access to God. Even the most eloquent writers on the subject are not agreed among themselves on this vital issue. Taking the Christian point of view, according to St. Paul, the soul wears a "celestial" or "spiritual" body in the other world as distinct from the "natural" and "terrestrial" body on the earth. "Flesh and blood cannot inherit the kingdom of God," he says. St. Augustine, however, declares that "in the resurrection the substance of our bodies, however disintegrated, shall be entirely reunited." He further clarifies this statement in these words: "Far be it from us to fear that the omnipotence of the Creator cannot, for the resuscitation and reanimation of our bodies, recall all the portions which have been consumed by beasts or fires, or have been dissolved into water, or have evaporated into the air."

Among modern writers also there is a grave divergence of opinion about this issue. "I believe in the resurrection of the flesh," says Bishop B. F. Westcott, "the flesh of which we speak as distinct to a resurrection is not that material substance which we can see and handle, measured by properties of sense." Dr. Fosdick affirms the persistence of the personality through death, but rejects the resurrection of the flesh, admitting, however, that he cannot easily imagine a completely disembodied existence. According to Dr. S. D. McConnel, the soul builds up, as it were, a brain within a brain, a body within a body, something like the "astral" body, which can persist after death. Bishop Manning is, however, more definite when he says, "When I enter there I shall be myself. This personality, these tempers and tastes, this character that I am forming here will be mine there. . . . I shall be seen as myself and shall be judged by what I am. I shall know my dear ones in the other life. I shall see and be seen. I shall speak and be spoken to." There are other views and opinions too. These citations have been reproduced as a sample to show that the state of man after death and the nature of the other world are still the objects of controversy and conflict of views even among the believers. *Where then lies the truth?*

The same divergence of opinion, in even a more prolific form, also exists among the Hindu authorities, both ancient and modern. According to Samkhya, there are innumerable souls which on embodiment are ruled by Karma from birth to birth. According to Shankara, every human soul is Brahman itself, indivisible and entire, oblivious in embodied life to His sovereign nature under the influence of Maya, an unexplainable conditioning factor which brings the whole creation into existence not as a cosmic reality but as an illusory appearance. Ramanuja, another famous philosopher, opposes this view and holds that the soul, or Jiva, is not identical with Brahman but subordinate to it. Swami Dayananda, a modern sage, believes, on the strength of Vedas, in the existence of innumerable spirits or souls who bear the fruit of Karma from birth to birth, until they attain liberation by righteous actions and worship of God.

The views expressed about the Hereafter and the nature of the Soul are almost as varied as there are sects or creeds in India. There are many who after the death of a person prescribe monthly or yearly ceremonies, known as Sraadha, in which offerings of food, drink, and apparel are made to the priest, who performs the ceremonies, in the belief that they reach the departed souls in the other world. There are other authorities for whom such ceremonies are not only useless but even constitute a flagrant violation of common sense.

In Islam too there is great diversity of views about the conception of the Hereafter. According to some authorities, the righteous soul after death comes to God and lives in blissful proximity to Him, while according to others he first enjoys the reward of his meritorious deeds in a delightful paradise. According to one school of Buddhism, there is no immortal soul, persisting unaltered through the endless circle of births and deaths, but rather the human personality is the result of an aggregation of material elements, known as skandhas, which persist as an integrated unit of life by the force of Karma, disintegrating again at the time of final dissolution, or Nirvana, on the expiry of past Karma brought about by a righteous way of life.

Others believe in an individual soul and its persistence through the dreary circle of births and deaths. Taoists have other views, and Zoroastrians still other. It is needless for our purpose to recapitulate all of them. Suffice it to say that there are almost as many views about God, Soul, and the Beyond as there are faiths and creeds in the world. This at the present state of man's knowledge and achievements is a very unsatisfactory state of affairs; as incommensurate with his mental stature as the stories of fairies and gnomes, appearing real to children, are for adult minds.

I should like it to be borne in mind that I am not pointing out these discrepancies in the religious beliefs of various faiths of mankind with any intent of criticism, as I hold religion and, in general, every healthy faith in such esteem and reverence that even the thought of destructive criticism would not enter my mind, but it is absolutely necessary to point out this variation to bring into prominence the errors that have been made in dealing with what is perhaps the most powerful incentive to noble effort in the heart of man. There are variations not only in the conceptions of the Soul and the Beyond, but also in the gospels of various faiths. Not infrequently the revealed teachings and commandments of one creed flatly contradict those of another, although both claim their origin from the same Divine Source. Is it possible that the Author of this vast Creation can be so variable and fanciful that He would say one thing to one, another to a second and yet another to a third and so on, thereby inciting one to fight the other on the basic issues of life and death?

There are many exponents of faith who gloss over these glaring discrepancies, arguing that every teaching is meant for a particular place, time, and people, the incongruities between them being inevitable. In their zeal to justify the stand that all these Revelations have emanated from God, they forget the obvious truth that there are divergences even in respect of basic issues like for instance the nature of Soul, the concept of the

Ultimate, the ideas about the Afterlife, and so on, which, being eternal Truths, could not have one form for a Hindu, another for a Christian, another for a Zionist, another for a Muslim, and an altogether different form for a Buddhist.

When in the case of physical knowledge, gathered by the puny, fallible intelligence of man, there is uniformity in our ideas about the shape of the earth, the phases of the moon, movements of the heavenly bodies, the nature of tides, the distance of the sun and moon, the flow of blood or the like—in which the variations, if any, are extremely slight—is it not inconceivable that the Revelations made directly by the Infallible Source of all Knowledge and Wisdom, the Lord God Himself, should be so conflicting and self-contradictory about the fundamental concepts of faith, which are not possible of verification by our senses and the mind? Not only this but some of the Revelations, like for instance, those dealing with cosmogonal issues and the Origin of Man, are found to be mythical and erroneous when studied in the light of the discoveries made by science.

We cannot also ignore the fact that every major faith is split up into numerous sects and creeds; and each of these divisions has its own ideas and concepts, differing from each other, but all founded on the authority of the Revealed scriptures, interpreted diversely to support the views expressed by the Founder of each sect. "Diverse are the Vedas [revealed scriptures] and diverse the Smritis [manuals of law]," says Mahabharata. "No sage was ever born who did not found a new creed. The essence of Dharma is shrouded in mystery. That by which great men travel becomes the Path." This ancient observation is applicable to any religion and faith and to any epoch of time. There has been, perhaps, no period in the history of mankind when there were so many cults and creeds and such a diversity of views about the Soul and God as exists in this enlightened age.

The main reason for this schismatic tendency in the domain of faith is that there is no unanimity of thought among the adherents of various faiths as well as among the adherents of each major faith. This diversity of views, in turn, springs from the blatantly obvious fact that the law underlying spiritual phenomena and the religious impulse in man has so far baffled all efforts to understand it. It is easy to infer, when viewed in the light of the fact that the physical universe is rigidly bound by laws from the movements of atoms to those of colossal suns and nebular systems, that there must also be a similar coherence and consistency in the spiritual realm.

It is also obvious that the human intellect, which discerns order in the cosmos, both in its tiniest fragments and the whole, cannot itself be devoid of system and law. It is deplorable that our present concepts about religion and its Founders savor of irrationality for the simple reason that when we hold that God himself revealed a certain gospel to a particular individual, in exclusion of the rest, we at once attribute nepotism and partiality to a system of existence ruled by inviolable laws from one end to the other.

There was a time when no thinker, however great, had the temerity to question the accounts of creation and cosmogony contained in the scriptures. This was not restricted to one faith but applied to all the religions of mankind. We are all aware of the historical instance when Galileo, white-haired and bent with age, was made to recant his monumental discoveries in the realm of astronomy by the dignitaries of the Church. Stringent punishments and the severest public opprobrium awaited those in India who dared to infringe upon the caste restrictions. Al-Hallaj suffered martyrdom for giving honest expression to his own remarkable spiritual experience, similar to that of many Yoga saints, because it was not in conformity to the orthodox faith. There can be no greater disservice to mankind at this crucial state than to belittle the decisive role played by religion in keeping man on the path of virtue and in diverting his thought to noble and sublime ideals of existence; but at the same time there can be no greater betrayal of the trust reposed by the masses on those who profess knowledge of the Occult and the Divine than to ignore the need of the time, demanding investigation of the laws underlying religious experience and phenomena, as has been done with signal success in respect to the phenomena of the physical world.

We are face to face with a colossal problem when we try to knit together the infinitely scattered threads of religion, say from the time of Moses to the present day. There is such a huge mass of literature, said to have emanated in part from God, and there are so many varied points of view that it appears impossible to untie the tangled skein and to locate the thread which now by winding and twisting reflects the appearance of an inextricably confused mass. It is needless for me to say that the difficulties I have pointed out in understanding the mysteries of religion and in lending belief to the various dogmas and beliefs have been felt by the majority of intelligent people at one time or another, though they often refrain from giving expression to their feelings for various reasons. A large part of them stifle their doubts and misgivings to avoid the adverse opinion of those who believe implicitly in faith, while others, swayed by sentiment, feel reluctant to cast doubts on the ideas and beliefs held by their parents and forebearers for centuries, and yet others continue to attend the Church and temple more to observe a formality than to satisfy a deep yearning of the heart that comes from a firm conviction in the tenets of a faith.

Frankly speaking, the intellectual stature of the average man has grown so high, as compared to his prototype of a few centuries ago, that the beliefs and dogmas of faith which instantly appealed to the latter now fall flat on the ears of the former. While there can be no gainsaying the fact that various religions of mankind, even in their present form, have a strong appeal for millions upon millions of their followers and keep alight the flame of spiritual knowledge even at this time, we cannot ignore the equally, if not more, important aspect of the matter that every fresh addition to the knowledge of mankind in the realms of biology, cosmogony, or psychology steadily adds to the ranks of the skeptics year after year until a time is reached when the present-day organized religions are reduced to mere skeletons, incapable of making any impact on the multitudes.

I am sure that the leaders of religious thoughts of all denominations visualize this catastrophe but feel themselves helpless to prevent it. We have already seen with pain how but one stroke of revolution swept away every trace of organized religion from the countries which came under its effect, with the result that, in the short span of half a century, the intelligentsia of these lands are now as antagonistic to the idea of God and the basic tenets of religion as they were in favor of them before.

# II.

# THE ERROR OF SCIENCE

ADDRESSING MYSELF NOW MORE PARTICULARLY TO THE SCIENTISTS and scholars, I may be permitted to say that there is absolutely no reason for self-complacency, much less for pride, in the thought that the intellectual efforts of the past two or three centuries have culminated in a vast increase in human knowledge, in a remarkable leap forward in technology, in political freedom, in the conquest of disease, victory over famines and progress in other directions conducive to the peace and happiness of mankind. I have purposely employed a note of caution for the reason that there are still large gaps in our knowledge, especially in the knowledge of human mind, which if not filled up, at least to the extent possible now, might result in undoing in a day all that has been achieved with the sweating labor of hundreds of years.

Leaving apart the lacunae in our knowledge of the physical universe—the increasing problems posed by astronomy, the real nature of time and space, the basic substance of the nebulae or the ultimate form of matter—it is no exaggeration to say that our present knowledge of the mind and its instruments, the brain and the nervous system, is still in its infancy, utterly insufficient as compared to the information we have gathered about the physical world. This disproportion in the knowledge of the two worlds in which we live, the outer and the inner, makes us a giant in one direction and a dwarf in the other, a clear sign of abnormality that cannot but have serious repercussions on our thoughts and actions, and thereby on our whole life and the environment that we create for ourselves.

If we have not so far realized the obvious truth that the zest for life and the happiness of mind flow from the inner fountain of our being and not from our material possessions, then we are still lacking in the proper understanding of our own nature. The birds in the air and the beasts in the forests live joyously and contentedly in the environment provided by nature. Because of his more developed nervous system and brain, and a more sensitive, unprotected flesh, man needs some amenities, it is true—wholesome food, shelter, and dress—but beyond these basic needs he does not depend much on his outer belongings for the possession of a joyous inner world.

Let us examine this issue a little more in detail. Can there be any denial of the historic fact that for the past thousands of

13

years a vast majority of the race has drawn consolation and solace at times of acute mental distress and despair, found inspiration and guidance at times of darkness and doubt, gained relief from pain and suffering, obtained peace in sorrow and grief, contentment in penury and want from the recorded or orally transmitted utterances of some famous men and women, whose needs were few and earthly possessions meagre but whose inner fount was so full of the greatest treasures and the noblest attributes of life that to this day they prove an inexhaustible source of strength and happiness for millions upon millions of human beings? When we look at the simple lives of the Founders of all major faiths, the Biblical prophets, the seers of the Upanishads, Socrates and Confucius or others, and the environments that surrounded them, we cannot resist the conclusion that luxury and overabundance are not at all necessary for the bloom of the inner man. From the experience of the past we can even say that their absence is more in harmony with the still unknown laws that govern the moral and spiritual development of man.

Can we deny that even the highest intellects of this age, men and women whose names are household words, at times of mental conflict much more prevalent now than it was ever before, continue to draw inspiration and strength from the lives and utterances of these simple, unassuming thinkers of the past? If not, is it not a matter for serious thought, much more serious than has ever been devoted to it? If with all our marvellous achievements in technology, tremendous advances in the arts and sciences and the provision of undreamed of luxuries and amenities we have failed in this glamorous age to produce even a few men and women, commanding the same stature, intellectual, moral, and spiritual, as was attained by most of these historical figures of the dim past in environments of ignorance, hardship and want, there must be something wrong with our own notions about human life and our own ideas about the measures needed and the environments necessary for the proper and harmonious development of man. How can any planning done in the present or the future prove fructuous unless we draw a lesson from this experience of the past and try to locate the serious gap in our knowledge that is making us progressively richer outside without adding a tithe to our treasure within? On the other hand, if we take stock of the world round us, we cannot fail to notice glaring signs and symptoms of inner poverty that is rapidly transforming mankind into a live volcano which with the least accident or indiscretion can burst to spread complete devastation not only on itself but on every form of life inhabiting the earth.

At the commencement of the present century, Professor Tyndall made what he thought was a remarkable statement when he said that he could see the possibilities of life in matter. Before him stalwarts like Cabanis, Buchner, Hobbes, Priestley, Comte, Mill, Herbert Spencer, Heckel, Karl Marx, and after them Freud, Santayana, John Dewey, Bertrand Russell, and others with all the power of their genius in their own particular spheres of thought directly or indirectly denied independent existence to life and consciousness. The influence of their thought persists to this day on the thinking of the scholars of our time, with the result that but few scientists of repute have the inclination to associate themselves openly with societies or groups interested in the occult and the supernatural. The irony is that all these mighty edifices of materialistic or agnostic

15

thought have been built up when matter itself is still a riddle and when nothing positive is known about the nerve impulses, about psychic energy, and about the bewildering activity of the nervous system and the brain. In the ancient civilizations of Greece and India atheists and agnostics flourished side by side with sages and visionaries, as incisive in their analysis and as logical in their arguments as are their counterparts today, but they never were able to stifle the deep-seated urge in the human heart that finds expression in religious ideas and acts.

No one can deny the greatness of these brilliant luminaries of the past, but at the same time no one can deny that some of the basic concepts about mind and matter on which they built their towering structures are now decade after decade eroded by fresh waves of thought, and the day is not distant when with complete erosion they will crumble down, surviving only as curious relics of a less informed past.

What are the fruits of this overemphasis on the soma, on unrestricted material amenities, on luxurious living, on the race for possession and power, and on the denial of the spiritual nature of man, or the independent existence of consciousness or an Almighty, Intelligent Cause of the universe we see around us? Has the human race become more noble, more happy, and more peaceful than it ever was in the past or do we notice ominous fissures and cracks in the huge mass that threaten an immediate collapse, and are not these ominous signs also in evidence in the wealthy, advanced nations at the zenith of material prosperity, surrounded by a plethora of all the lavish blessings provided by science? What inner torment drives millions upon millions of young men and women to seek solace in hallucinatory drugs, in ceaseless smoking, in alcohol, while millions more, tired of ordered life, roam from place to place as hippies and tramps, as rebels to society, often in a state of total abandonment, utterly indifferent to the rules of conduct and modes of behavior that are sacrosanct for the elder generations? Why do millions more in all walks of life take to occult practices, to spiritualism, to astrology, asceticism, to Yoga and the like, in unprecedented numbers in an effort at self-transcendence to find answers to questions that no amount of temporal knowledge can answer or to assuage a hunger that no hoard of material wealth could ever satisfy in the past? Can we shut our eyes to the glaring fact that in no period of history, even during the darkest age, were there such atrocities, such wholesale massacres, such hideous wars and such bloody revolutions as this century has witnessed? And after witnessing all this horror, is there a single country or a single nation on earth that does not prepare for war? Or is there any that is not every now and then torn by internal dissension or shaken by revolts, upheavals and bloodshed that make a stable environment or a regular life well nigh impossible?

I am not in any way attempting to paint a gloomy picture of the over-all condition of the modern world. Flagrant disregard of moral values, indecency, indiscipline, violence, sexual delinquency, and the like have assumed a position of ascendancy that is grossly reflected in most of the newspapers and periodicals of the day. Before the very eyes of many of those whose writings or discourses dismantled the walls that were erected by faith to keep man from yielding completely to the animal in him—time-honored conventions, higher rules of conduct, chivalrous ideas, the ideals of family life, affection and love, chastity and rectitude, altruistic and philanthropic zeal, lofty codes of honor—all those sublime attributes of character that distinguish man from the beast—are crumbling to dust amid the laughter and derision of the nihilists and the anti-Christ. The last days of the Romans, the most luxurious nation the world ever saw, were marked by certain characteristics, mentioned by historians, which can serve as a warning about the fate in store for the glamorous civilization of our time. They were: (1) The breakdown of the family, (2) The mounting craze for pleasure, (3) Extravagant spending, (4) Expanding armies and constant threat of attacks, (5) Depreciation of moral values, (6) Decay in religion, (7) Political instability and (8) Immoderate sex.

Considered in the light of this fact, who can doubt that modern society is rapidly heading toward the same ignominious end, and the ominous signs and symptoms that cause some degree of alarm in the sober and the sage are but the forerunners of serious calamities to come? It is a historical fact that no once victorious nation and no once powerful dynasty of kings in the past ever came to a realization of the fact, when degeneration set in, that they were decaying and rapidly rolling down the slope, until one day they landed in the mire at the base. On the other hand, they ascribed their growing problems and troubles to their enemies, oblivious to the fact that the real enemies were their own fast deteriorating minds. The writers, thinkers, rulers, spiritual heads, and scholars of today, irrespective of the country or the nation to which they belong, seldom realize that by conforming to the taste and choice of the masses they cannot arrest the process of decay, for the reason that degenerative tendencies in art, literature, philosophy, social customs, national character, moral values, and even in religion remain unnoticed by those who fall victims to senescence.

While the leaders of religious thought continue to dwell on the blessings of faith, both from the pulpit and in the press, in masterly works and discourses, the ranks of unbelievers continue to swell or new creeds and cults continue to spread, leading to chaos and confusion which become more confounded every day. In the same way, the politicians haranguing on peace see violence growing apace, and the moralists, lauding the path of virtue, watch in despair the advancing tide of immorality, powerless to stop it.

What has suddenly gone wrong with the world? Why do the erudite find themselves powerless to cope with the growing spate of violence, discontentment, and disaffection spreading on all sides? The Communist countries are as much flooded by it as the rest of the world. Even an optimist like Julian Huxley has had to admit that there is a bright future for humanity provided it does not destroy itself in a nuclear war. This is the frame of mind of most other thinkers and scientists as well. But why this pessimism? Why are the promises held by science and technology proving to be a source of worry and fear rather than that of elation and joy? And this is just the beginning. What will be the aftermath of the third World War, if it is fought? Do not all signs and portents point to the conclusion that sooner or later a global conflagration is inevitable? What will be the condition of humanity when, devastated by nuclear blasts, a battered and broken remnant survives, amid the ruins of modern civilization, to carry on the task of history? Can any one provide answers to these questions, and can any one visualize to what harvest the present waves of unrest, revolt, violence, bloodshed, depravity, and disorder would lead? If not, does it not mean that the fate of mankind hangs by a thread, and all the resources and ingenuity of the race are now powerless against the threatening monster that has been raised, and that for this we can only blame the faulty thinking and planning of the architects of the modern world?

It is not correct to say that this discordance is due to the transition from an agrarian to an industrial state of society or from a rural to a predominantly urban life, surrounded by conveniences provided by advanced technology, and that a certain duration of time would be needed for mankind to adjust to it. It is equally wrong to say that all these unhealthy reactions —violence, war, revolt, delinquency, drugs, and the like—are the outcome of lack of adjustment on the part of individuals to their unconscious urges and impulses that are normally suppressed. Equally incorrect is the argument of the men of faith that all these evils are the inevitable fruit of heretical tendencies and the revolt of reason against God. The stand that vice and wickedness were always present in human nature and they appear more widespread now, as they are coming out more in the open, owing to the present greater freedom of thought and act, is equally fallacious. Experience of the past does not support any of these arguments. Barring the one single factor of the influence of modern technology, which alone cannot be so pernicious, all the other factors (urbanization, suppression of unconscious urges, heresy and unfettered freedom of thought and action) also operated in the past without causing such explosive situations—social, moral and political—as we are witnessing now. Social, moral, and political evils assumed overwhelming proportions only when a nation or people, through a wrong mode of life and thought, fell victims to decay, a grim process of inner deterioration leading finally to senescence and death—the award of Heaven on a collective breach of evolutionary Laws. *This is the verdict of history.*

The greatest tragedy of our time has been that, carried away by the overwhelming impact of important discoveries made in the domain of science, the thinkers of this age, believing that they had found solutions to most of the riddles that confronted them, gave expression to views about the various facets of human life, about the hopes and aspirations of man, about his mind and spirit, about the aim of his existence, about this world and the Hereafter, which in many important respects are as incorrect as were the concepts of the ancients about the physical world. The gravest error in this assessment has been the summary dismissal of religion and the supernatural as a phenomenon not verifiable through the methods adopted by science and, therefore, not worthy of inclusion in the province of scientific research. One of the main reasons responsible for this uncompromising attitude of science toward religion rests partly on the dogmatic attitude of the custodians of faith themselves, insisting on blind acceptance of the teachings contained in the gospels of a creed, and partly on the exaggerated stress on divine intervention and theophany that characterizes more or less all the religions of mankind.

A more considerate assessment, however, would not have omitted to take cognizance of the fact that there is no other single factor, including politics, that had such an influence on the life of man from the remotest antiquity to the present day as religion has wielded, and no other factor that has contributed so richly to the growth of civilization and culture as it has done. An institution or a bent of mind that has persisted for thousands of years in all the vicissitudes through which mankind passed could not rest on mere fancy or delusion or fraud or a bubble created by the priests, but on something more solid existing in the mental fabric of man. It certainly could not be a pathological or hysterical affection for the reason, firstly, that in such a case it could not have persisted through all the stages of human growth from the most primitive to the present cultured state and, secondly, if such were the case, then it means that the loftiest men ever born had this mental kink in a more acute form than is the case with common men. Such a premise, in turn, would lead to the preposterous conclusion that the highest achievements of thought with respect to the nobler aims of life are only possible in a disordered condition of the human brain.

That prejudice has been the main cause responsible for this failure to investigate one of the most prevalent and most constant phenomena of the human mind is obvious. Even a casual study of the major faiths of mankind could not fail to bring home to any unbiased scholar that, according to all schools of religious thought, a certain prescribed way of life and conduct and certain prescribed mental and physical disciplines can act as a ladder to lead earnest seekers to God or to states of consciousness in which communion with Divinity becomes possible. This systematization of religious effort to gain sublime objectives is at least as old as history, and no doubt was practiced in almost all countries under the sun. The religious lore of India is especially rich in this respect, and it is not at all difficult, even for a casual observer, to see that from time immemorial hundreds upon hundreds of highly venerated sages and seers bore unrebuttable testimony to the efficacy of the various methods and disciplines prescribed for the purpose of granting the spiritual insights and the super-normal gifts associated with religion in any form. Later on, these methods and disciplines came to be known under the generic name Yoga, and under this appellation continue to this day. During recent years, Shri Ramakrishna, Maharishi Ramana, and Shri Aurobindo, three outstanding products of this ancient culture, also bore unreserved testimony to the efficacy of these systems and the extraordinary experiencs that flow from them.

The most rational way to attest the truth of religion, and to accept or reject its claims, was to give a trial to these practices and disciplines after making a comparative study of all the systems in existence in different parts of the earth, and then to pronounce a verdict on the basis of the results achieved. But to this day it was never done by any group of scientists, dedicating their life to this research alone, in the same way that innumerable groups and societies are doing in respect to the still unexplained riddles of the physical world. The decision to ignore the claims of faith and to refuse its admission into the province of science was thus taken without trial, a most unscientific way to deal with an obstinate phenomenon of this type. The Society for Psychical Research came into existence to investigate another category of phenomena, relating to paranormal manifestations in certain specially gifted individuals, which are not explainable in terms of the known laws of science. Even this research, undertaken in a skeptical environment, yielded valuable information and proved decisive in establishing the validity of telepathy or, in other words, the possibility of communication between two minds directly without any known interconnecting medium to make the communication possible. Premonition, prophesy, and clairvoyance, though not conclusively proved, showed a high degree of probability, and the weight of evidence in respect to physical phenomena — telekinesis, levitation, materialization, etc. — was such that the possibility could not be ruled out altogether.

But there was no investigation of the possibilities offered by religion itself. The utterances of the spiritual luminaries of the past, treated with great reverence for thousands of years, were rejected outright without trial. It became the fashion to explain the phenomena of mind in terms of atoms and molecules composing the matter of the brain. The more sanguine are looking forward to the day when they can manipulate the genes to produce human embryos at will. Others visualize the production of test-tube babies at not too distant a date. Every word that a scientist writes is to be accepted as gospel truth. But every word in a scripture is to be viewed with doubt, and distrust. The wheel of fortune that once gave such ascendancy to faith that it became the sole arbitrator of what a man should believe or not believe, irrespective of the evidence of his senses and the judgment of intellect, now turning round has reversed the position and made reason the arbitrator, alas, to be guilty of the same abuse. The summary condemnation of religion as unworthy of attention of men of science, as time will show, has been one of the most colossal blunders ever made by man, because under the loose and sometimes fantastic dress, worn by faith, lies concealed the greatest secret of existence, which rules the fate of mankind in the same way that the gravitational pull of the sun governs the rotation of the earth.

The ancient scriptures of India, studied with attention, will be found to be full of references to this still unknown Spiritual Law. The entire religious literature of the world will be found to be an expression of this mighty Law, intuitively grasped by the prophets and sages of the past. Not only in the Shruti (that is, the revealed scriptures, for example, the Vedas) but also in the Smritis (the manuals of Law) and in the Puranas (that is, mythology) the nature of this Law and its implications and possibilities are discussed again and again, embellished with supernatural accounts and episodes which prevent the uninitiated from reaching the solid core. There is undeniable evidence to show that this secret was initially discovered in some remote civilization prior to the entry of Aryans into India, for there are unmistakable signs to show that it was known to the denizens of the Indus Valley civilization three thousand years before the birth of Christ. To avoid ambiguity, I should like to say at once that it is a biological Law, as possible of demonstration in a laboratory as the flow of blood. The tragedy is that the specialists and the scholars of today treat the human brain like a sealed compartment, as circumscribed in its performance as the brain of an animal. Although there is undeniable evidence to show that in certain specially constituted individuals, as for instance in the case of mediums and sensitives, mystics and seers, child prodigies and even men of genius, the normal human limit is exceeded to an amazing extent, in a manner for which there is no satisfactory explanation from the side of science, the scholars, moving in the same old rut, continue to harp on the bewildering complexity of the brain and the enormous number of brain cells as a sufficient cause to account for any paranormal phenomena exhibited by man. This means, in other words, that scientists of this category are adopting the same dogmatic attitude toward the still inexplicable phenomena of mind as ecclesiastical pundits adopted toward the unintelligible physical phenomena a few centuries ago.

# III.

# EVOLUTION IS
# THE ANSWER

THE OBVIOUS EXPLANATION THAT THE HUMAN BRAIN is still in a state of evolution and that these extraordinary phenomena, witnessed in these uncommon men and women, are but the erratic manifestations of a higher state of consciousness that will be the natural possession of the man of the future may still not find favor with the biologist, but this explanation provides complete corroboration for and squarely fits in with his own theories about the origin of man. The phenomena are erratic and often beyond the control of the individuals themselves, for the simple reason that there is still a wide gap between the present condition of the human brain and the ultimate state of perfection it has to reach when only these, what we call supernatural or paranormal, gifts can become the normal possession of at least the fully evolved members of the race. Till that time, in the great majority of those who are born with these talents as a natural heritage, we can reasonably expect only imperfect, erratic, or abortive exhibitions, as we see in mediums, psychics, and even in some categories of mystics, on account of the fact that the combination of circumstances and the eugenic factors involved cannot but continue to remain faulty in the present state of the society, now in utter ignorance of this mighty Law. There is, however, no doubt that by an incredible combination of factors finished specimens of the perfect man of the future were born at rare intervals, as in the case of Buddha, Christ, Vyasa, and others, who, endowed with a superior type of consciousness and in possession of paranormal gifts, amazed their contemporaries with their extraordinary psychical and intellectual talents which the latter, ignorant of the Law, ascribed to special prerogatives from God.

The same phenomenon must have been repeated during the period of transition of the anthropoid into man, and abortive, unfinished specimens of the intelligent man to come must have commenced to appear now and then. They exceeded the highest limit of the general mental level of the sub-man, until finally the transition was complete, having been assisted from time to time by the superior contributions of the latter for more healthful ways of life and better organization of society. From the dawn of history, the illuminatti effected a better organization of human life and society much in the same way by their example and precept to facilitate the process of evolution till the summit is reached. The explanation for the amazing tenacity with which mankind has held fast to the teaching of prophets and sages, even at the cost of widespread bloodshed and suffering—a mysterious phenomenon that has defied all attempts of a rational solution so far—lies in this, that the teaching in one form or the other, to a greater or lesser extent, contains precious hints about the mode of life and the organization of society necessary to meet the demands of the evolutionary impulse still active in the race. This teaching, emanating from exalted states of consciousness, the natural endowment of the man of the future, seeing further ahead than the intellect, was accepted as Revealed, as it is not the product of a normal mind, but of a consciousness still far beyond the capacity of the normal human brain.

In dealing with religion and every supernormal manifestation of the human mind we are, therefore, dealing with the phenomenon of evolution, in extremely rare cases resulting in the appearance of men and women who exhibit in a miniature or imperfect form one or more of the extraordinary talents that would be the normal adornment of the future man. In all probability, in the prehistoric days in India or even in some earlier culture, the symptoms attending the abnormal conditions of mystics and mediums were carefully studied by the contemporaries to understand the reasons for the extraordinary states. The usual explanations that the manifestations were the result of possession of the individuals by a spirit or demon or a divine being, even when readily accepted, still left the primitive inquirers wondering how the possession could occur; and naturally the physical symptoms which attended the manifestations must have been observed with equal care to find the secret of the strange exhibitions, showing possession of powers and gifts entirely beyond the capacity of the average man. The most common feature of this mystical phenomena, entrancement, is often exhibited in varying degrees by mediums also. According to the observation of Meyers, "during the trance, breathing and circulation are depressed. The body is more or less cold or rigid, remaining in the same position which it occupied at the oncoming of the ecstasy, however difficult and unnatural this pose may be. ... A swoon-like condition is also present among certain types of hysteria as also among mediums and sensitives during seances." It is easy to imagine that time and again the more enterprising among the primitive observers of these strange exhibitions must have tried to induce the same psycho-physiological conditions in themselves—insensibility, diminished breathing, and a cataleptic condition of the body—with the aid of different methods in which restraint of breathing (in imitation of the born cases), now known as Pranayama, must have played a prominent part. During the course of these amateurish trials, a most remarkable coincidence must have occurred somewhere with the appearance of the strange phenomena in one already mature to some extent for the experience, resulting in the discovery of one of the greatest secrets of nature hidden in the body of man. That secret is Kundalini.

Space does not permit me to dwell on this discovery in detail. For a further exposition of all the available material several volumes would be needed, which will appear from time to time. Suffice it to say here that this fabulous Power Reservoir, referred to in the Vedas, the oldest recorded religious scriptures in the world, as Gayatri, the cornerstone of every spiritual and occult practice and the one, single source of all mystical experience and

paranormal phenomena, has been the most sought after object
of quest in India for the past thousands of years. Adept after
adept in unambiguous terms has testified in recorded confessions
to the existence and efficacy of this marvellous psychosomatic
Power Mechanism with awe and adoration and has treated it
as an All-Intelligent and Omnipotent Divine Energy, the archi-
tect of every form of life in the universe. What is of particular
interest, with special relevance to the problems of this age, is the
fact that in hundreds of these writings the biological reactions,
caused in the body on the arousal of the Power Center, have
been described in unmistakable terms, the best that general level
of knowledge of those days allowed the authors to do. They provide important clues for the modern investigator who has even
a passing knowledge of physiology. These accounts are so numerous, so consistent, so unmistakably pointing to the same experience, despite variations in time and place, and often so sin-
cere in their expression it is a wonder that the momentous nature
of the discovery has escaped the keen eyes of the modern scholars,
both of the East and the West, who studied and translated some
of these works.

Although a good deal of the intricate mechanism of the human body has become known through the laudable efforts of
modern savants, it is still an unfathomed mystery, even to the
most erudite scholars of our age. The province of thought especially is still the most inscrutable realm of all. So deep is the
mystery and so unprepared for the disclosure are the learned that
hardly anyone would be ready to believe the amazing truth, that
as a measure of evolution a subtle process is at work in the average
human body, resulting in the formation of a biochemical essence

of a volatile nature that can be readily transformed into a psychic radiation of high potency. From a rational point of view no unbiased man of science should feel incredulous of such a possibility, for the simple reason that in every form of life the production of nerve and psychic energy is constantly going on to feed the brain and the nervous system, although the manner in which this is effected, the nature of the energies and the method of their formation from the gross ingredients of the organism are yet not known to science. What I aver is that the process of evolution leads to the production of a more potent form of those biochemical substances that act as fuel for psychic energy in its various forms. It would be ridiculous to contend that the most elaborate chemical laboratory on earth, that is, the human body, cannot readily manufacture a substance of this nature, under the influence of evolutionary impulses active in it. In an infinitesimal dose of a three hundred thousandth part of a gram, equal to a speck of dust, lysergic acid, diethylamide, popularly known as L.S.D., creates a revolution in human consciousness, and may even lead in rare cases to insanity, suicide, or murder, an apparently incredible performance for such a minute dose. Scientists cannot trace what happens to it in the body but can recognize its action by its results. On this analogy is it unreasonable to suppose that the human body has in it or can manufacture a substance so subtle that it cannot be detected with any of the present methods of examination, and yet so potent that in the form of radiation it can raise the human consciousness to such higher levels of cognition where other planes of existence and other orders of being come into the range of perception of an individual?

What is of particular importance in this issue is the fact that the existence of this biochemical substance and its transformation into radiation, either as a natural measure or under the effect of certain practices and disciplines, is not to be taken purely on trust but can be observed and verified under the most rigid laboratory conditions in certain categories of men; and the observation can be repeated time after time until the Law is formally recognized. I am emphatic on this point on account of the fact, firstly, that I have myself observed the entire phenomenology of this experience for more than thirty years within myself and, secondly, the experience is confirmed not in a few but in hundreds upon hundreds of authentic documents dating from prehistoric times not only in India but in Tibet, China, Japan, and the Middle East also. The documentary evidence is so overwhelming that no reasonable man can disbelieve it even for a moment. Why it has not already created a revolution in modern thought is primarily due to the fact that many of these precious documents are written in what is known as Sandhya Bhasha, or twilight language, that is, in the cryptic form, which though plainly intelligible to one who has had the experience is often Greek to the noninitiate. With the elucidation that will be attempted in the works in hand on the subject, not only these enigmatical passages but also the veiled allusions to the changes resulting from an awakened Kundalini in the scriptures and other sacred lore of India will become readily understandable. Considering the volume of the ancient literature available on the subject in India alone, it would take a team of scholars several years to decipher the obscure writings even with the aid of the key furnished.

The question that now rises is how can the phenomena relating to Kundalini be demonstrated conclusively to meet the

33

demands of scientific research, even admitting that the documentary study can provide convincing material in their support? The answer to this question is simple, for it is precisely in this aspect of the problem that my own experience, though attended by awful suffering at times, has been of invaluable assistance to me, as if purposely designed to initiate a poor, mediocre man like me into the mystery. What my own experience has clearly revealed is the amazing fact that though guided by a Super-Intelligence, invisible but at the same time unmistakably seen conducting the whole operation, the phenomenon of Kundalini is entirely biological in nature. Probably no other spectacle, not even the most incredible super normal performances of mystics and mediums, so clearly demonstrates the existence of an All-Pervading, Omniscient Intelligence behind the infinitely varied phenomena of life as the operations of a freshly awakened Kundalini. It is here that man for the first time becomes acutely aware of the staggering fact that this unimaginable Cosmic Intelligence is present at every spot in the Universe, and our whole personality—ego, mind, intellect, and all—is but an infinitely small bubble blown on this boundless Ocean; and to suppose that even a particle of this Ocean of Consciousness can ever become extinct or cease to be is more absurd than to imagine that there can be night on the sun. "From that lake (Ocean of Life) in which not even a mustard seed can find room (that has no dimensions)," says the Yogini Ialla, "all living creatures drink water (have their existence). From it deer, jackals, rhinoceros and sea-elephants (all forms of life) are born and into it they sink."

With the awakening of Kundalini, an amazing activity commences in the whole nervous system from the crown of the head to the toes. In Hatha Yoga, the activity coincides with the proficiency gained in Pranayama in the case of successful initiates, normally extremely few in number, but the operation is so gradual that it is hardly perceptible in the primary stages. In the case of those whose nervous systems have already attained a state of maturity, as a fruit of favorable heredity, the awakening can occur abruptly, whether effected by Raja Yoga or Hatha Yoga methods or by any other discipline, making use of concentration as the lever to achieve the aim. Whenever an awakening of this kind occurs, the normal biological rhythm of the body immediately experiences a drastic change, entirely beyond the power of control of the Sadhaka. His body is now transformed into a miniature laboratory, working at high speed day and night. In the Chinese documents this phenomenon is described as the "circulation of light" and in the Indian manuals as the "uprising of Shakti (life energy)." The nerves in all parts of the body, whose existence is never felt by the normal consciousness, are now forced by some invisible power to a new type of activity which either immediately or gradually becomes perceptible to the Sadhaka. Through all their innumerable endings, they begin to extract a nectar-like essence from the surrounding tissues, which, traveling in two distinct forms, one as radiation and the other as a subtle essence, streams into the spinal cord. A portion of the essence floods the reproductive organs which, too, become abnormally active as if to keep pace with the activity of the entire nervous system. The radiation, appearing as a luminous cloud in the head, streams into the brain and at the same time courses through the nerves, stimulating all the vital organs, especially the organs of digestion, to adjust their functions to the new life introduced into the system.

The awakening of Kundalini denotes, in other words, the phenomenon of rebirth, alluded to in plain or veiled terms in the religious lore of mankind. A more powerful and direct connection is now established between the individual and universal Consciousness, and the body, obeying implicitly new impulses and directions, communicated through Prana, the interconnecting biological medium, acting on itself, takes up an amazing process of rejuvenation, aimed to overhaul the nervous system and the brain, until a new type of consciousness or, in other words, a new inner man is born. The narration of the whole process would need a volume in itself and will be taken up in another work. It is sufficient to mention here that during the whole course of this transformation, in addition to the blood and other fuels present in the body, every particle of the powerful reproductive fluid in the system is sucked up through the spinal canal to irrigate and feed the various nerve junctions and the brain. This entirely biological operation is carried out in such an unmistakable way that even a novice in physiology cannot fail to notice it. The semen in men is now produced in such abundance that a tiny stream rises day and night through the spine into the cranium to provide the richest and the purest food for the now heavily overworked brain cells. In women, the sexual energy and secretions involved in erotics are used as the fuel. This is a perfect example of the forethought and the ingenuity of nature to keep the body equipped with all the necessities to make the completion of the evolutionary process, normally needing eons to accomplish, possible in the short span of one life. The tonic food provided by seminal essence, now manufactured in rich abundance and reaching every part of the brain with the cerebrospinal fluid, nourishes the brain cells and the nerve fibers, stimulating them to higher activity necessary for the emergence of a more enlarged consciousness than was manifested before.

This phenomenon of transformation or rebirth is alluded to by Christ in metaphorical language in his dialogue with Nicodemus when he says, "Verily, verily, I say unto thee except a man be born of water and of the spirit, he cannot enter the Kingdom of God. That which is born of the flesh is flesh, and that which is born of the spirit is spirit. Marvel not that I said unto thee, ye must be born again." Among the Hindus the term "twice-born," applied to the higher castes, entitled to wear the sacred thread which has three strands, symbolic of the three nerve channels of Kundalini, only refers to the possibility of the same spiritual rebirth in them. It is amazing that a momentous concept on which the whole structure of the Hindu society was built in the Vedic age should have lost its true significance through the vicissitudes of time. The emphasis on chastity, or Brahmacharya, common to most religions, is clearly rooted in the fact that, in the case of earnest seekers after illumination, the need for the preservation of seed is imperative to meet the exigencies of the awakening. Viewed from any angle, the cult of Kundalini will be found to be the bedrock of all genuine religious experience, known in many parts of the earth to the spiritual adepts of the past. By a strange irony of fate, this vital knowledge is more scarce today, in this enlightened age, than in all the other periods of history. This is how nature retaliates to the arrogance of man.

There is an erroneous conception among certain ranks of scholars that transmuted seed is the direct cause of spiritual experience. As is readily understandable the human seed itself is built of two components: the gross organic substances and the subtle

Prana, or life energy. About the latter we are entirely in the dark at this stage. This Prana is not the product of the reproductive machinery alone but is distilled from the whole body by the nerves. It is this pranic essence extracted by the nerves, countless in number, which, as a radiation, streams into the brain on the awakening of the Serpent Power. This more potent nerve and psychic energy, circulating in the system now, flows directly to the spinal cord and the brain, giving rise to the strange and weird phenomena that characterize the arousal of Kundalini in the initial stages. The grosser substances are used for the purpose of extra nourishment demanded by the cerebrospinal operation theater to carry the evolutionary processes to a successful termination. The unrestricted opportunity for sexual gratification allowed by nature to man has, it is obvious, a most important reason behind it. The precious organic substance and the concentrated energy, present in the seed, instead of being ejected for a momentary pleasure, can also be used, when the rejuvenation process is at work, as a tonic nourishment for the nerves and the brain cells in order to effect a metamorphosis of the inner man. By no other external feeding known to science can this wonderful transformation be brought about.

While it can be readily conceded that, with the present methods of observation, the transformation occuring in the consciousness of the initiate cannot be detected, even with the aid of mechanical devices, there can be absolutely no denial of the position that this is strictly a biological phenomena. For instance, the intense activity of the sexual organs is clearly perceptible in the case of men. The ceaseless flow of the reproductive substances into the spinal cord, the vital organs, and the brain, and also the altered activity of the digestive system and even of the heart at times, can be easily observed with the help of the information available in the ancient literature on the subject.

The statements of the kind that during the process the shukra (semen) dries up with suction or becomes thin, that the male organ shrinks, or that the sexual appetite is lost, contained in the old manuals, cannot fail to convey important bits of information to the modern savants engaged in the investigation. An ancient Chinese work, "The Secret of the Golden Flower," contains unmistakable hints about this process, which no one with some knowledge of the subject can fail to notice, and yet Jung, in his commentary on the book, entirely preoccupied with his own theories about the unconscious, despite the unambiguous nature of the statements in the work, finds in it only material for the corroboration of his own ideas and nothing beyond that. The same thing happened in a seminar held by him on Kundalini of which a written summary is still available in the Jung Institute. Not one of the savants present, as is evident from the views expressed by them, displayed the least knowledge about the real significance of this hoary cult and the tremendous import of the ancient doctrine they were discussing at the time.

# IV.

# THE MECHANISM OF EVOLUTION

IT IS EASY TO INFER THAT IF PARANORMAL ACHIEVEMENTS and a transcendental state of consciousness are possible for some men they must be possible for others also, provided the biological factors at the base of the manifestation, in the case of the former, are present in the latter too. It is impossible to believe that God or nature can be partial to those who possess the gifts and endow their minds with these extraordinary attributes as a mark of special favor. A more rational explanation for the phenomenon, unless we choose to adopt a dogmatic attitude, would be to ascribe a biological cause for them and to find out by study and experiment where the secret lies. No one can deny that human consciousness itself is the expression of a biological organ and that, apart from the organism, it is never perceptible in any form. Is it not, therefore, but rational to assume that for any wide departure from the normal pattern of consciousness, there must occur a corresponding alteration in the biological machine also?

Fuel for normal activity of the human brain is not, as is sometimes supposed, supplied by blood alone. The real fuel of thought is the psychic energy supplied by a limited number of nerves after extracting it from various parts of the body. On the awakening of Kundalini the entire nervous system is soon harnessed to the task, with the result that a more powerful fuel, in the form of radiation, streams into the brain, enhancing its activity to such degree that a highly extended consciousness, which has an overwhelming effect on the initiate, now wafted to other planes of existence, replaces the old, narrow, sense-dominated awareness that never could rise beyond the strictly circumscribed limits.

The main hurdle in the way of an empirical demonstration of the change in consciousness lies in the fact that no method has yet been devised to determine the nature or potency of the psychic energy used by the brain. The moment this is achieved the verification of the subjective phenomena, as for instance the enlargement of consciousness, would also become possible. At the present moment we have absolutely no method to determine the variation in the nature of consciousness of a genius and a common man, though this difference both in the volume of awareness and the nature of the psychic energy used is always present.

Until the nature and properties of Life-energy, or Prana, serving as the fuel of thought, is determined by science, the modern savants will continue to be baffled by the phenomena of mind and consciousness in the same way as the ancients were mystified by the aurora borealis, lightning, thunder, and the like, until the mystery was solved by the discovery of electricity. The most practical way to study this elusive substance, more marvellous than any substance of the physical world, is to investigate the phenomenon of Kundalini. With the present highly developed methods of observation, once the clue is found it would not be difficult to follow the track with patience till conclusive data about the new field of research is collected. The domain of consciousness is, however, so amazing that there will be no cessasion of mysteries and surprises for even the most powerful intellects till the end of time.

Positive evidence about the inner changes can, however, be furnished by the successful initiates themselves even at this stage. They have already done so in hundreds of memorable cases in India and other countries. These accounts can leave no one in doubt about the surpassing nature of the metamorphosis that is effected. The change occurring in the consciousness can never be imagined by one who has not had the experience. It is the stupendous nature of the vision which is at the root of the idea in the mind of a person who undergoes the experience that he is beholding a Super-human Being, or a Super-human state of Existence, surpassing everything he knows, including the whole universe. It is therefore no wonder that those who had the vision all through the past believed they were beholding the Creator Himself. During recent years Tennyson, Wordsworth, Marcel Proust, Bucke, and others had experiences somewhat similar to those of mystics, under different circumstances, without undergoing those rigorous disciplines usually associated with spiritual unfoldment. When regular research is started, it will be found that also in the past this "gratuitous grace" has been a common feature of mystical experience, as if those who had it were already fashioned for it from birth or needed but a slight stimulus to gain it.

The extremely diversified accounts of religious experience are due to the variation in the mental level, ideas, and cultural development of those who have it. For a thorough investigation of the phenomenon it is necessary that a team of scholars and scientists, comprising skeptics and believers both, should take up a course of exercises for a sufficient period in a spirit of dedication, as is done for other scientific objectives, with due regard to the ethical standards necessary for it. And then they could evaluate the results.

Even one case of awakening would be sufficient to determine the biological nature of the phenomenon, and to observe the various changes and developments that occur. The metabolic processes of the body are highly accelerated, and an inner process of brain building and streamlining, somewhat akin to the processes occurring in an embryo in the womb, takes place until consciousness is completely transmogrified and a superior type of mind is born. What achievements are not possible with an awakened Kundalini, once the feasibility of the transformation is empirically demonstrated and the biological factors involved become known to the men of science? It can be readily imagined to what levels of perception the brain can be raised when it is constantly fed, during the process of renovation, by the most powerful nerve food not obtainable by any other means, prepared by the reproductive organs in amazing abundance under the impact of a newly generated activity completely unknown to science.

It is not at all necessary to depend entirely on the accounts of those under discipline about the inner changes experienced by them. There are unmistakable external signs also by which this change can be detected and even measured. When transformed, the initiate must become a genius or a virtuoso of a high order, with extraordinary power of expression, both in verse and prose, or extraordinary artistic talents. Some of the ancient prophets and seers are the historical examples of this metamorphosis. Precognition, powers of healing, psychic talents, and other miraculous gifts may develop simultaneously along with genius. A modern intellectual with a healthy constitution and noble attributes of character can bloom into a spiritual prodigy, a man of such extraordinary gifts and talents that he can shine as an idol before the admiring eyes of the multitudes, with a power of fascination and appeal possessed only by the most magnetic of men. In this way the metamorphosis effected can bear striking testimony to the efficacy of processes generated by Kundalini. I am making these statements with full responsibility about the accuracy of what I say, and there are countless volumes to support my assertions in every detail. The explanation for the metamorphosis is not hard to accept. The evolutionary mechanism is so constructed that at a certain state of maturity it can be stimulated to such intense activity by means of appropriate methods that the evolutionary cycle can be completed in one's lifetime, raising man to the next higher stage of consciousness decreed for him by Divine Ordination.

There is absolutely no difficulty in a scientific investigation of the phenomenon when the spheres of its operation are known. The biological reactions in the body are unmistakable. The ceaseless suction of the seminal fluid and its flow into the spinal canal, nerve junctions of the vital organs, and the brain cannot remain undetected. The symbol of an erect organ of generation in some statues of deities in India is indicative of Urdhava-retas, or of this upward streaming of the reproductive essence for effecting transformation of consciousness. The phenomenon is so ancient and so widespread that it is amazing modern science has no inkling of it even now. The halo or aureola shown round the heads or figures of saints and illumined sages is symbolic of the inner illumination experienced on the metamorphosis of consciousness. There is a noticeable change in the digestive and excretory functions of the body during the course of the transformation.

There are other developments that can be pointed out to the investigators when a research project is taken in hand. It is obvious that from both the subjective and objective sides, the phenomenon is as possible of verification as any other function of the human body. The point that now rises is why should such an overwhelming importance be attached to this research, when the ultimate object of the awakening of Kundalini is merely a change in consciousness which, as the past record shows, can be effective only in an extremely limited number of cases, and therefore the phenomenon cannot be of importance or interest for the whole of the race? The futility of the question becomes obvious when we recollect what giant revolutions in human life and thought were effected by the handful of spiritual geniuses born in different parts of the earth during the historical period. This factor alone presents a phenomenon of such magnitude that it makes research on Kundalini a pressing need of the times. But there are many other equally important factors which when taken together make Kundalini virtually the arbiter of human destiny and, for that reason, by far the most powerful driving influence on the life of man.

Another important factor in this series is the decisive role played by Kundalini in providing an avenue for the satisfaction of the deep-rooted religious impulse in man. We are all aware of the fact that the urge to experience the transcendental or to solve the riddle of our being is, to a more or less extent, present in most men, and in some cases it assumes such an overwhelming proportion that it becomes the most powerful guiding influence in life. Even the skeptics are not without the desire to solve the mystery of creation. But no attempt made by the intellect, assisted by all the inventions of science, can penetrate the veil, because the veil itself is the creation of the intellect. It is only by self-transcendence that light begins to penetrate into the darkness, dissolving the problem, as shadows melt at the approach of dawn.

This elevation of consciousness can only occur through the transformations brought by Kundalini and by no other agency human or divine. The present rapid multiplication of sects and creeds, which the orthodox custodians of the various faiths are powerless to stop or even to account for, owes its origin to the mounting pressure on the brain caused by the religious urge, the inevitable fruit of civilization and leisure, which only an awakened Kundalini can ease. The millions upon millions of men and women who seek solace in occult practices of any kind, in Yoga, in drugs, in prayer and worship or in any other form of spiritual effort and eagerly hunt for teachers and adepts for guidance are, often without knowing it, yielding to a subconscious urge to rouse Kundalini, an urge almost as powerful as that which makes a healthy young woman long for a child. Even in the Communist countries in the next few decades, the ever-increasing pressure of the inexorable evolutionary processes will break the fetters forged by a political ideology, ignorant of the law, that suppresses healthy expression of the religious impulse and, if this outflow is still denied, may result in the same violence in finding a vent as was previously used to prevent it. History will follow in the reverse direction unless the Law is recognized and obeyed.

Let us now come to another equally important aspect of Kundalini. With all the knowledge provided by modern psychology at our disposal, we are now in a position to guess correctly what can be the outcome of denial, suppression, or distortion of a deep-rooted natural impulse present in the mind of man. We are already aware of the unwholesome effects caused by the denial or suppression of other deep-rooted natural tendencies, like the reproductive urge and the maternal instinct. On this analogy would it be wrong to suppose that the same results can follow from the suppression or denial of the religious impulse and that they too can lead to mental unrest, depression, perversion, disorder in the system, abnormal behavior and in extreme cases to insanity?

Since Kundalini is the fountainhead of the religious desire in man, it means that a mode of life and conduct or a system of society that puts a brake on its legitimate activity can never be conducive to peace and happiness but must, on the other hand, lead to psychic and physiological disturbances both in the individual and the group. The religious impulse, unlike the reproductive urge, is not static but dynamic in its operations. In other words, it is not appeased by the same kind of nourishment over and over again but demands a change in diet, according to the evolutionary stature and the intellectual acumen gained, and when this is denied it gropes blindly for other vicarious foods to satisfy the hunger gnawing inside. The multiplicity of creeds in this age is, therefore, nothing to be wondered at. The tendency will continue to spread until the right food is found.

Mental disturbance and psychosis are, at the present state of our knowledge about this nerve mechanism, not infrequently the possible consequences of a sudden arousal of Kundalini. This possibility has always been recognized by the specialists in this science. In the ancient pictorial representations, the Goddess is always shown making the sign of dispelling fear with one of her hands. Fear is one of the most common symptoms of neuroses and psychotic conditions. The initiation ceremonies in India and Tibet and the hideous practices, such as sitting astride a corpse for meditation, resorted to in some cases, are merely crude methods to fortify the mind of the initiates against the unimaginably frightful phases of the awakening. It should not be difficult to understand that the practices aimed to arouse the Serpent Power sometimes result in abruptly forcing open the central channel and the connected compartment in the brain at a time when the system is not yet attuned to such a development. In such cases terrible ordeals await the initiates, through which only some survive. It is easy to imagine that rapid flights to higher levels of consciousness, as is envisaged in every form of Yoga, cannot be without some degree of risk—unless the mind and body have been attuned to them by appropriate methods, including proper cultivation of the will-power—for seekers who take to them with all the earnestness at their command.

Taking now another feature of religion, we find, as I have pointed out in the opening lines of this dissertation, that primitive religions were a bundle of superstition, revolting forms of worship, savage ritual and myth. Since the evolutionary impulse is a part and parcel of the psychosomatic organism of man, and not any miraculous influence exerted by God in chosen cases nor a thought wave created by any prophet, it is only natural that the expression of the impulse should correspond to the psychological level of the people. Therefore we should not expect the religion of the barbarian and the savage to have that refinement and sublimity that permeated throughout the historical period of the civilized nations. And yet at the same time we cannot expect that the religious concepts and ideas prevalent thousands of years ago would continue to hold the same attraction and appeal for a higher intellectual level of people. Revolt in some form against the obsolete ideas and forms of worship or ritual is, therefore, just a natural outcome of the psycho-mental evolution of the race. The inexorable march of time must cause the same revolutions in the spiritual sphere as it has caused and is causing in the social and political fields to conform to the evolutionary needs of mankind. All cramping influences can only prolong the agony of resistance to an unavoidable advancing tide. The mushrooming growth of countless novel cults and creeds is indicative of the first impact of the tide and the eager search of the masses for a more satisfying spiritual food than the one provided by the older faiths.

We now come to the most important aspect of Kundalini. It can be readily understood that the evolutionary impulse cannot be active only in the individuals but must be operative in a collective sense as well. The influence of evolutionary processes on the ecological development of a whole species or group is now clearly recognized by the biologists. It is obvious that in order to meet the needs of the evolutionary growths, changes in the environment—social, political, and moral—would be necessary from time to time to meet the demands of the developing psycho-mental fabric of the individuals and of the race too. Where this adjustment is delayed, causing a retardation in growth, revolts, revolutions, and wars intervene to effect, with widespread suffering and bloodshed, what could have been achieved by peaceful means provided the underlying Law were known and its mode of operation understood. Constant violation of the Law and the prevalence of social, moral, and political conditions not in conformity with the evolutionary needs must, at last, lead to ceaseless turmoil, senescence and decay. The ancient civilizations, cultures, and empires, after attaining a certain level of ascendancy, fell victims to decadence as the lives of the people did not conform to those standards—political, moral, and social—that were demanded by the mental stature attained as the fruit of evolution at the time they touched the zenith of their career. The sudden or gradual eclipse of the ascendant nations of the last few centuries was also brought about by the same causes. The degenerative tendencies that have now set in among almost the whole of mankind as the consequence of modern defective ways of life, incommensurate with the present evolutionary stature of the race, owe their origin to the same factors. No amenities provided by science, no new spate of inventions, no psychological cures, and no amount of education can arrest the growth of this canker unless the evolutionary demands are fulfilled. The danger to the race from a continued neglect of these conditions in the present state of technological development is too plain to escape the notice of even the least observant. But the reason why effective measures are not employed to end it, is that the present habits of thought have become too ingrained to be changed, a last symptom of decay.

It is a historical fact that all the founders of the existing major faiths of mankind and all great prophets, mystics, and seers, who claimed to have won access to Divinity in one form or the other, were almost all of them men and women of extraordinary intellectual acumen, and most of them were credited with the possession of the miraculous gifts of prophesy, clairvoyance, control over the elements, healing power, and the like. It is also well known that miraculous powers have always been associated with prophets and saints from prehistoric times, and even in this age the general belief is that accomplished Yogis, saints, and other spiritual men in some way gain contact with and even power of control over the subtle forces of nature, beyond the reach of common men. We have already seen that the high-potency psychic radiation, produced by Kundalini from the marvelous chemical laboratory of the human body, is the common source of all the supernormal states of consciousness common to prophets, seers, and mystics of all categories. Since genius, high intellectual calibre, and miraculous gifts are a common adornment of the mystic mind, it is but logical to conclude that genius and miraculous powers also owe their origin to the operations of Kundalini. From this it follows that the highest intellectual and artistic talent (such as in the case of men of genius and virtuosos—and psychic or miraculous powers, in the case of mediums and sensitives or others possessing the gift of healing or other psi faculties without the visionary state of consciousness peculiar to mystics and seers) also flow from the same source. In actual fact, this phenomenon provides valuable circumstantial evidence in support of the stand that Kundalini is the evolutionary energy and mechanism in man. It is only a process of evolution that can lead to the extraordinary formations of the brain biologically necessary for the exhibition of talents and gifts entirely beyond the capacity of normal brains. Taking into consideration the transformation that has been wrought in every sphere of human life and thought by a few hundred talented and gifted men, through all of history, can there be any line of research more important and more beneficial for humankind than that which would show the way to tap the amazing source that showers these priceless gifts, thereby making cultivation of genius a practicable achievement for man?

The question that arises here, as a natural sequence of what has been stated, is that if the Serpent Power is the source behind genius and high intellectual or artistic talents it must also be the factor responsible for the evil geniuses of history, the highly talented military commanders, dictators and demagogues who drenched humanity in blood, and also for the human monsters who, dead to every moral sentiment, with their proclivity and genius for crime, commit such dreadful acts which make the horrified readers of their gruesome exploits shiver with fright. This is the malignant or destructive aspect of Kundalini, symbolized by the ancient Indian savants in the form of Kali, who, black in color from head to foot, is depicted with her mouth dripping with human blood, a severed human head in one of her hands and a garland of skulls round her neck. In her benign form Kundalini is Durga, the creatrix, the dispeller of ignorance and all evils and ills. In her malignant form she is Kali, the Goddess of destruction, often the tutelary deity of those engaged in nefarious activities, thugs, dacoits, black magicians, and the like. It is incredible that a vital secret concerning the existence of a biological device in the human body that has the capacity to raise man to the stature of a god, with supernormal gifts and virtues, like saviours and sages, or the capacity to fashion him into a monster, as in the case of the human scourges of the past and present, which has been known in India for centuries, should still be a sealed book to the luminaries of this age. It is this ignorance of an awful secret of nature that has exposed mankind to the horror of terrible wars, revolutions, inhuman suffering, and shattering loss during the current century. No amount of material wealth and prosperity can save mankind from the depredations committed by highly gifted, amoral men, pursuing ambitious goals, in whom Kundalini is awake in a malignant form. Their hold over the masses being irresistible, their power of organization unmatched, and their military skill unequalled, even one specimen of this class, in the present state of technological knowledge, can play havoc with the whole of humanity and all it has achieved during the last many thousand years.

The only silver lining in the dark clouds threatening mankind at present is the recognition by science, after a thorough investigation, of this almighty Law. The race can no longer afford (now or in the decades to come) to play with fire and allow her own ignorance of the awful Law to result in the continued birth of evil geniuses, fatal to the survival of the race. The point now arises as to how a divine power, designed to lead the race to unimaginable heights of glory, peace, and happiness in the outer world and to transcendental states of consciousness in the inner, can be so diverted from its natural course that it produces virtual monsters for the destruction and torment of the race. The answer to this very relevant question is not hard to find. It is the ignorance of the Law and the lack of cooperation on the part of the surface consciousness with the hidden operations of the evolutionary force that are at the bottom of the catastrophe. All the Revelations made by the known prophets of the past, to a more or less extent, contain precious hints about the ways of life to be followed to avoid resistence to or obstruction in the process of evolution which, as always happens in the case of violations of any natural law, can be disastrous both for the individual and the race. It is very well known that man needs a certain complete and balanced diet to insure freedom from disease and a smooth, efficient functioning of the system. For the purpose of proper, harmonious growth of the body and the mind nature provides a ready-made, easily digestible food for the human infant, complete in all respects in the mother's breasts. In the same way, the transformative processes of Kundalini need a certain healthy and harmonious condition of the body and the mind to compound in proper proportions the subtile essences that form the fuel for the high-potency psychic radiation which is at the

54

bottom of all extraordinary or supernormal exhibitions of the human mind.

A wrong mode of life, disharmonious social and political environments, improper food and drink, immoderation, and intemperance, and also excessive worry, anxiety, and fear, unrestricted ambition and desire, greed, selfishness, envy, jealousy, and hatred, in fact all those attributes of mind that have been condemned as evil by the revealed knowledge of mankind, acting adversely on the system, interfere directly with the proper manufacture of the precious fuels, with the result that the psychic radiation, lacking healthy nourishment, takes on a stunted, distorted, or diseased form, in the same way that lack of proper food in insufficient measure stunts, distorts or damages the health of a suckling babe. This is the reason why Revelation came to guide mankind. Like the nature of the Law, its enormous implications and effects were and are even now unknown. Every prophet and seer born on earth came, in fact, knowingly or unknowingly to draw attention to this occult Law. The signs and symptoms of degeneration that we notice now, and which marked the closing phases of all the premier civilizations and victorious empires of the past, point conclusively to a deterioration in the physical and mental assets of a people or nation, causing an impoverishment in the quality of the evolving psychic energy, leading to those deficiencies, faults, and flaws which are characteristic of decadence in the rising generations and those yet unborn. Decline in moral values, family affection, conjugal love, or in the ideas of loyalty and fidelity or the standards of truth, honesty, patience, and perseverance, absence of originality, lack of the sense of responsibility and self-restraint, intemperance, immoderation, and indolence are some of the characteristics of the decadent mind.

Disproportion, deformation, or distortion in the psychic radiation is the cause of the appearance of not only the sadistic geniuses, who cause horrible slaughters from time to time, but also of many forms of neurosis and insanity. Professor Zaehner in his book, "Mysticism, Sacred and Profane," has touched a very important point in citing the instance of John Custance, a certified manic-depressive, who is prone to mystical experiences during his manic-periods. Similarly Huxley in his work, "Heaven and Hell," has cited the case of Renee, a schizophrenic who has given an autobiographical account of her own passage through madness. She calls the world of the schizophrenic "the country of lit-upness," as Huxley writes, of which the illumination for her is infernal—an intense electric glare without a shadow, ubiquitous and implacable. The summer sunshine is malignant, and so on. The subject is too vast to be dealt with in this short summary, but from my own experience and from a study of many cases that I have come across, both in India and in the West, it is obvious that the awakening of Kundalini in a person not well adjusted to it, with defective organs or an unhealthy nervous system or a faulty heredity or any other flaw, which research will disclose, leads to hysterical, neurotic, or insane conditions of the mind. The liability to mental disorder in the case of those who take to Yoga or other forms of religious discipline is recognized both in India and the Middle East. Those who stumble on the path and survive with some form of mental derangement are caller "Mastanas" in Persian, as opposed to "Farzanas" of the sober class. Psychotics of this category in their lucid intervals exhibit clairvoyance or other paranormal faculties despite of their abnormal behavior at other times. I have come across several cases of enlargement of consciousness in Europe, arising from an active Kundalini. Some of them, though possessing lofty traits of character and even, at times, psychic gifts, because of an unfavorable environment or other reasons are variable in their moods, and instead of experiencing that spontaneous ever-abiding joy which a gracious Kundalini bestows, also pass through periods of depression. The growing flood of mental troubles, which is a curse of modern civilization even among the more advanced nations, is nature's forewarning that the evolutionary process is going wrong. The relation of schizophrenia to puberty in a vast majority of cases has a special connotation in the light of what I say.

It is not necessary for me to emphasize the paramount importance of the disclosures I am making. I have presented this summary to make the enormous implications of the doctrine of Kundalini clear beyond doubt, as I have found by experience that even among the intellectuals only a very few, blessed with intuition, have been able to grasp them in their entirety. What I emphatically assert is that one single Law is at the base of all, at the present moment, inexplicable phenomena of the human mind. Only one remarkable series of changes, caused in the psychic energy that serves as fuel for thought, is responsible for all the varied and complex phenomena that present at this time insolvable riddles to science. The greater incidence of insanity among the men of genius and the seeds of eccentricity in many of them (considered in the light of the fact that the danger of madness is ever present in any effort directed to arouse the

Serpent Power) clearly establishes the existence of a common link between the two. Research into Kundalini implies, in fact, an investigation into almost all, at the moment, obscure phenomena of the mind.

The investigation carried out by the Society for Psychical Research and other allied groups or individuals on mediums, sensitives, clairvoyants, psychic healers, Yoga practitioners and the like has not yet been proved conclusive, for the reason that in this way the investigation is directed to the innumerable branches and leaves of a giant tree of which the root is Kundalini. It is far more practicable to take hold of the root to make a study of the phenomenon than to examine the branches and leaves to find a solution to a problem that becomes a hundred times more intricate there. In dealing with mind and consciousness we deal with a different type of energy and a different plane of existence than that known to us through our senses. It is a recognition of this fact that is decisive in launching a research into the occult. This is the base from which a real study of the cosmos begins, for the universe we see is real only in the human state of consciousness. Beyond that it is reduced to a mirage in the dimension just one step higher to it, denoting the tremendous difference caused by a change in the potency of the psychic radiation effected by Kundalini.

Although I am as sure of the fact that all the numerous developments I have mentioned proceed from the working of Kundalini, that is, from the operation of one, single, at the moment hidden Law of nature, ruling the world of life, as I am of my own existence, yet I must say with all the emphasis at my command that every word I have said should be first weighed in the scale of reason, then rubbed on the touchstone of the recorded experiences of the past, and finally tested in the crucible of research before the least credence is placed on it. I say so because a single false doctrine, widely accepted by the unwary, can at this stage do incalculable damage to human weal. One single Law, as I have said, is at the root of almost all the inexplicable phenomena, urges, and impulses of the human mind, like, for instance, the impulse to worship, superstition, desire for supernatural or spiritual experience, the awe of the numinous, belief in the super-mundane and the hereafter, super-normal faculties— precognition, clairvoyance, telepathy, prenatal memory, automatism, mental healing and the like, intuition, skill in astrology, palmistry, fortune telling, etc. genius, mystical experience, revelation, inspiration, neurosis, insanity, moral sense, aesthetics, piety, the rise and fall of nations, degeneration in individuals, families, and groups, evolution and its allied phenomena–all proceed from the operation of but one cosmic Law. From this it is obvious that the Law of Parsimony operates with equal force in the realm of the spirit also. And how could it be otherwise, for all the universe we see and all the law and order we perceive in it are but reflections of a plane of existence compared to which the sensory world dwindles to the likeness of a thin vapor floating across the surface of an ever-lasting, ever-bright, limitless sun. All extraordinary and supernormal psychic gifts, all extraordinary and abnormal conditions of the mind, all the desire for transcendental experience or for the vision of God or for a nobler and happier state of being and all the revolutionary ideas, both good and bad, flow from altered conditions of the psychic radiation, produced by Kundalini, as both light and darkness proceed from altered positions of the rotating earth.

# V.

# THE DIVINE
# POSSIBILITIES IN MAN

CHOSEN BY DESTINY, THAT RULES EVERY EVENT OF THE UNIVERSE, to make this fresh disclosure of an already discovered super-physical Law, in a manner incomprehensible to myself, because of my own limitations and human frailties, I do my utmost to draw the attention of the scholars of this age to the vital importance of a scientific investigation of the phenomenon. I know that the yet imperfect and incomplete account of this divine mechanism I have rendered in my writings can only kindle a spark in the darkness of doubt and confusion prevailing at present; but at the same time, I am confident that the labor and sacrifice of those men of science who, unconvinced by the existing theories about

mind, are following like sleuths the trail toward a real solution
to the problem and those individuals who, prompted by a divine
impulse, are striving day and night for a purer and better world,
will succeed in establishing the existence of the almighty power
mechanism of Kundalini, as described by me, to the satisfaction
of one and all. In answer to the question that the divulgence of
the secret of this awful Power might place in the hands of the
wicked a terrible weapon to harm the world, it is enough to point
out that save for the born cases, the arousal of Kundalini in one
whose mind harbors evil will invariably lead to insanity or death
and, secondly, that an open knowledge of the secret can act as
the surest safeguard against the misuse of the august power as
at least the well-informed section of mankind will have been
sufficiently educated to distinguish a diabolic product of this
kind, however eloquent and magnetic he might be.

I stand alone in the disclosures that I am making. There is
every likelihood that both from the sides of religion and science
eyebrows will be raised and open doubts expressed at what I say.
This will be only a transitory phase, as every important discovery
in the realm of knowledge almost invariably took the world by
surprise. But when the destined hour arrives, circumstances so
transpire that, however incredible the disclosure might have
appeared in the beginning, soon after a day comes when it becomes the most talked about topic of the day. In my humble view
there is nothing that can counteract the overhanging threat of
nuclear holocaust like the knowledge of Kundalini. Once the
possibility of a spiritual rebirth with the arousal of this mighty
power is accepted by mankind, Kundalini Yoga will provide the
most sublime enterprise for the pure-minded and intelligent
adventurous spirits of the age. To the share of this lofty class of

men, adorned with the knowledge of the inner and the outer worlds, will fall the herculean task of educating humanity in the essentials of this almighty spiritual Law to guide the race to the glorious estate ordained for it.

There can be nothing more antagonistic to the lofty concept of Divinity, as inculcated by most of the religions of mankind, than the idea that at any time in his long career on earth mortal man can attain to a state where he will have gained all the knowledge about the creation and the Absolute. The moment he begins to think in this vein he arrogates to himself a position of rivalry to the omniscient Creator of the Universe, a mark of arrogance which his knowledge of the physical universe should have driven out of his head long ago. Those who oppose a new idea or a new wave of thought without allowing it a fair trial clearly betray the presence of a lurking idea in their minds, born of pride, that they know all that can be known of the world. I, therefore, beseech all those who strive for a happy future for mankind, both from the ranks of scholars and men of faith, to put what I have said to the severest possible test they choose in the experiments conducted to prove the correctness of the hypothesis.

About the methods of awakening Kundalini, the precautions needed and the way of life to be followed by those who would like to offer themselves for this sublime enterprise, a good deal of information is already contained in the ancient manuals and some more would be added in the volumes that will appear on the subject from time to time. It is, however, necessary to point out that the present wave to equate mystical experience with the hallucinatory conditions caused by certain drugs or with hypnotic conditions induced by suggestion, guided meditation, or multisensory sound and light environments or by any other artificial means is the outcome of a most erroneous conception about the genuine mystical state. Resort to these artificial conditions, demanding no effort at self-mastery, is as dangerous to the evolutionary development of the human brain as the use of narcotic drugs by ascetics has been to the spiritual cause in India. Until the law behind mystical phenomena is established, attempts to imitate conditions of consciousness about which nothing definite is yet known can only be treated as apish. These methods have been employed from time immemorial to satisfy the itch of minds ravenously hungry for spiritual experience but whose mode of life and attributes of character stand in the way of real self-unfoldment. They are like the sweets containing opiates, used by unscrupulous nurses sometimes to put restless children entrusted to their care to sleep. The very idea of gaining access to God by means of chemicals, mental suggestion or some meditational technique constitutes a mockery of all the sublime teachings of religion that call on man to prepare himself for the supreme vision by adherence to lofty ideals of life. Those men of science and those teachers of spiritual disciplines who overlook this vital point in this way express denial of the need for moral elevation and enoblement in those who strive for spiritual enlightenment.

The finished products of Kundalini must transcend the normal limits of the human brain. If this transcendence does not occur, the visionary experiences are either a delusion or myth. Even those who have sporadic glimpses of the Ineffable but for a few times in their life are usually men of genius or of high intellectual stature. Those in a state of perennial ecstasy must essentially have uncommon intellectual talents, paranormal gifts, and an altered rhythm of the nervous system. In their case the enlarged consciousness persists even in slumber, for which reason such sleep is called "Yoga Nidra" or the sleep of Yoga. The marvellous Power Reservoir of Kundalini, the unmistakable symbol of the Divine in man, opens up new horizons of such sublimity, joy, and glory that even a modest description would appear incredible unless a few transformed adepts support my assertions to convince scholars of the golden future ordained for humanity. In no other period in history have the learned been so mistrustful of the divine possibilities in man as they are now, and in no other age has the need for spiritual geniuses been as urgent as it is at this time.

The human mind is so constituted that no luxury and no treasure of the earth can assuage its burning fever seeking an explanation for its own existence. All the heavy weight of this inscrutable mystery, all the questions posed by intellect, all the suffering of the harrowing ascent of evolution, all the pain felt at the injustice and misery prevailing in the world, all the disappointment of shattered dreams and broken hopes, all the anguish of eternal partings from near and dear ones, and all the fear of ill health, decay and death—vanish like vapor at the rise of the inner Sun, at the recognition of the inmost Self, beyond thought, beyond doubt, beyond pain, beyond mortality which, once perceived, illumines the darkness of the mind as a flash of strong lightning cleaves the darkness of the night, leaving man transformed with but one glimpse of the inexpressible splendor and glory of the spiritual world. May this sublime knowledge become accessible to all. May there come enlightenment and peace to the minds of all.

"... I have called you friends; because all things whatsoever I have heard of my Father, I have made known unto you."

St. John, Chap. 15

YOUR INQUIRY IS INVITED

Kundalini Research Foundation, Ltd.
440 East 62nd Street
New York, New York 10021